**Daring and vulnerable, this is the highly
anticipated new collection from Griffin Poetry
Prize winner Billy-Ray Belcourt.**

In *The Idea of An Entire Life*, Belcourt delivers an
intimate examination of twenty-first-century anguish,
love, queerness, and political possibility. Through
lyric verse, sonnets, fieldnotes, and fragments, the
poems—sometimes heartbreaking, sometimes slyly
humorous—are always finely crafted, putting to use
the autobiographical and philosophical style that has
come to define Belcourt's body of work. By its close,
the collection makes the urgent argument that we are
each our own little statues of grief and awe.

Praise for *The Idea of An Entire Life*

"To read Billy-Ray Belcourt's *The Idea of An Entire Life* is to experience genre as a place between landscapes, but also beyond them: horizon as 'line break,' infrastructure as 'wound,' 'an image of a forest someone else / was supposed to know by heart.' These poems are achingly beautiful. Belcourt writes what's already broken, breaking in real-time, 'in order to repair it.' How this new form might arrive, 'miraculously' but also diligently, an act of recuperation and courage that's on-going, 'meandering' but also (always) 'incomplete,' becomes what happens when we read."   —Bhanu Kapil

"This was beautiful. I am wowed, again. There were moments when I lost my breath. *The Idea of An Entire Life* engineers a lexicon for us to decipher what it means to be wedged between a staling futurism and the em dash of colonial chronicle. Where the body is a poem and the poetics of embodiment are found in grammatology: in the enjambment of a horizon 'between me and my / ancestors,' here a semicolon proceeds finality in asking 'What if when my life ends there is still more life?' and the queer Indigenous rite that with a huffing comma we 'continue living.' Belcourt creates a blueprint, mapped on waxy hard ground, the world the stylus etching out designs beneath: quotidian utopias, reverberant chambers, the portcullis of history, the choreography of a bedroom. And I too, like Belcourt, peek from the margins and of his sonnet weave a wave."

—Joshua Whitehead, author of *Making Love with the Land*

"*The Idea of an Entire Life* reaches toward the edge of language and returns to us a map of becoming. Belcourt offers us a vision where life might be something tender, magic, and deeply radiant."

—Jake Skeets, author of *Eyes Bottle Dark with a Mouthful of Flowers*

Praise for *This Wound is a World*

Winner of the Griffin Poetry Prize • Winner of the Robert Kroetsch City of Edmonton Book Prize • Winner of the Indigenous Voices Award for Most Significant Work of Poetry in English by an Emerging Indigenous Writer • Finalist for the Governor General's Literary Award for Poetry • Finalist for the Robert Kroetsch Award for Poetry • Finalist for the Gerald Lampert Memorial Award • Finalist for the Raymond Souster Award

"*This Wound is a World* is a decolonial wildfire from which the acclaimed writer Billy-Ray Belcourt builds a new world and it's the brilliant, radiant, f*cked up Indigenous world I want to live in. . . . [His book] redefines poetics as a refusal of colonial erasure, a radical celebration of Indigenous life and our beautiful, intimate rebellion. This is a breathtaking masterpiece."

—Leanne Betasamosake Simpson, author of *Theory of Water*

"This book is a monument for the future of poetic possibility. It is rare to be able to call a book something so grand and full—and have it be utterly true. That's what *This Wound is a World* affords us: myth and hyperbole pressed into a lived and realized life. A reckoning for and of the wreck—bravely buoyant, alive, and finally here."

—Ocean Vuong, author of *On Earth We're Briefly Gorgeous*

"*This Wound is a World* is a wonder. It is filled with humor, sadness, sadness about sadness, sex, profound and profane lyricism, and above all power. . . . The book is a world with worlds inside it. It means to de-colonize any possible reader's pre- or mis-conceptions about what it means to be alive and Indian today."

—Tommy Orange, author of *There There* and *Wandering Stars*

Praise for Billy-Ray Belcourt

"No one breaks your heart as elegantly as Billy-Ray Belcourt."
—Eden Robinson, author of *Son of a Trickster*

"Billy-Ray Belcourt is proving himself to be a literary genius. His poetry and prose are tender and brutal and brilliant."
—Heather O'Neill, author of *The Capital of Dreams*

"There are few writers who can authentically capture the beauty and complexity of Indigenous existence both on the rez and in the city like Billy-Ray Belcourt."
—Waubgeshig Rice, author of *Moon of the Turning Leaves*

"Billy-Ray Belcourt's voice is uniquely plangent and self-aware."
—Tommy Orange, author of *There There* and *Wandering Stars*

"Belcourt is the rare writer who composes from, to, and because of the soul." —Claudia Dey, author of *Daughter*

"Billy-Ray Belcourt uses a dexterity of language and form as a container for memory and nostalgia as vehicles for truth about a still-blooming present."
—Hanif Abdurraqib, author of *There's Always This Year*

"Belcourt crafts sentences like only a poet can, each one precise and shimmering. He writes with ferocious intensity and beauty about Grindr hookups, queer Indigenous friendship, police violence, the open wounds of Canada's residential schools, loneliness, and longing."
—*BookPage*

"Belcourt sheds light on the transformative potential of love."
—*Publishers Weekly*

the idea

of an

entire life

the idea

of an

entire life

poems

BILLY-RAY BELCOURT

raised voices

Beacon Press, Boston

Beacon Press
24 Farnsworth Street
Boston, Massachusetts
www.beacon.org

Beacon Press books
are published under the auspices of
the Unitarian Universalist Association of Congregations.

28 27 26 25   1 2 3 4 5 6 7 8

Printed in the United States of America
Published simultaneously in Canada by McClelland & Stewart
and in Great Britain by Carcanet Press Limited.

Typeset in Aldus Nova by Sean Tai

Library of Congress Cataloging-in-Publication Data

Names: Belcourt, Billy-Ray, author.
Title: The idea of an entire life : poems / Billy-Ray Belcourt.
Description: Boston : Beacon Press, 2025. | Series: Raised voices |
Summary: "A powerful meditation on the present as a space where the past
    and a still-possible utopia collide"—Provided by publisher.
Identifiers: LCCN 2025016195 (print) | LCCN 2025016196 (ebook) | ISBN
    9780807022405 (trade paperback ; acid-free paper) | ISBN 9780807022412
    (ebook)
Subjects: LCGFT: Poetry.
Classification: LCC PR9199.4.B448 I34 2025 (print) | LCC PR9199.4.B448
    (ebook) | DDC 811/.6—dc23/eng/20250509
LC record available at https://lccn.loc.gov/2025016195
LC ebook record available at https://lccn.loc.gov/2025016196

The authorized representative in the EU for product safety and compliance is
Easy Access System Europe 16879218, Mustamäe tee 50, 10621 Tallinn,
Estonia: http://beacon.org/eu-contact.

For my friends

CONTENTS

the idea

of an

entire life

How we exist in the world
depends on how we describe it.
Have I always been firmly in the world?
No: I've been autumn in the middle of August,
I've been happiest when my life feels
like autofiction. Alas, the twentieth century
never ended. *We are all subjects of the twentieth century*,
I say to a stranger I just met on the internet.
It sounds like a riddle for which the answer is the body.
There is a blank space inside all natives that history
lays claim to. Every winter, I take pictures of the snow
because the snow reminds me of my impermanence.
Mostly I want to be undone without being ruined.
A native truth: the present is as beautiful as it is brutal.

UTOPIA

Utopia is an impossible demand. Most likely,
it's what happens when no one's looking.

On Grindr, my profile stated: DESIRE IS A PLANET
TRAPPED INSIDE AN EVEN BIGGER PLANET.

The men I met were aroused by the world;
I was aroused by the opposite of the world.

Turns out there can be so much night
inside a single man that to be contained

within it is a kind of violence. Turns out the body
is so much more than I ever bargained for.

Of course I didn't love them properly—I lived
with the vastness and loneliness of a continent.

Please don't ask me to define love.
All I have is a second language.

Nothing is truly inexpressible.

Picture the women waiting at the forest's centre, their hands folded into little coffins.

Not even the snow falls with such imprecise hunger.

In time, love deranges all of us.

In time, all love is reduced to the childlessness of music.

(A painting of a palace with six hundred rooms; in each a mechanical bull, thronging violently.)

Most days, my job is to work out the difference between truth and honesty.

True or false: we are a closer catastrophe than heaven.

ENDNOTES

About semantics, too much has been made
of the difference between mourning and melancholia.
I have stood at both sides of a long decade
and my grief took the shape of the same arrow
clenched between the same dead boy's teeth.

*

In my country, death is a door that swings open.
Onto all the trees in the neighbourhood, I wrote:
UP CLOSE A NATIVE IS A DEMONSTRABLE
IMPOSSIBILITY.

*

When I told my kokum I was homesick,
she said: *If heaven is a place, my dear,
I'm afraid it's already underwater.*

*

Unsurprisingly, the past makes me
painfully available to the world.[i]

*

A human body is reminiscent of a sentence
in that it too can taste like dust.

*

What do I want from literature, anyway?
A new way of living, a new way to talk
about the trees that doesn't endanger them.

AN ENTIRE LIFE

for Brenda Draney

When I said *the instabilities of the self*
reveal the publicness of our emotions

I meant that loneliness is a kind of season;
it falls on us like rain. Maybe the body

really is a necessary fiction. Once, in a hospital,
my gallbladder malfunctioning, I saw the arc

of my entire life and there was an equal amount
of joy and heartache and somehow I still loved

the idea of An Entire Life. I was in a room
with people who knew everything about me

and all I could think about was the burden of blue
and the indistinctness of spring. There was so much

I hadn't yet written about. Brenda, I've been meaning
to tell you: my favourite invention is my mother.

She believes in angels and second chances.
I believe in the magnificence of a lake in northern Alberta

and the radical possibilities of telling strangers
all my secrets. What do you make of the aspen trees,

by the way? Oh, how their leaves tremble
even when the world is completely still—

I, for one, am really no different.

*In a letter dated July 24, 1935, from the Office of the Indian Agent
at Driftpile, Alberta, an Indian Agent—a government henchman
who enforced the Indian Act, a piece of legislation that, for
example, forbade the practice of ceremony as well as the use of
Indigenous languages—describes a Cree man's attempt to rescue
his children from an Indian residential school.*

I.

During this era, reserves were, in effect,
open-air prisons. When you live
in an open-air prison, even the rain feels
like a slap from God.

2.

The mind is an absent ruler.
It is a shape I try to fill in.
Most days I am as hungry
as a shoreline.
The lake is my ancestor,
even if it will outlast me.
I am serious when it comes
to desire, if only because
a man is a difficult thing
to dwell inside of.

The letter describes the seizure of the "monthly rations" of the family of J.B. Gambler, "an Indian of Calling Lake," who made fugitives of his children when he hid them from the bodysnatchers at an Indian residential school in Wabasca. Gambler didn't want the state to "regain possession" of his children and transform them into its wards; he didn't want to surrender his family to the process of making-property that was colonial education. Gambler swore at the Indian Agent and threatened to shoot him dead. In response, the Indian Agent marshalled the extra-legal power of the state: he made use of its monopoly on torture and withheld food. I don't know what happened to Gambler or his children, whether or not they were, in the end, stolen from him again. The letter doesn't (and can't) tell us anything about Gambler as a father who loves his children.

4.

The surname of the Indian Agent
is the surname of a man who pays
my mosum to repair his vehicles.
My mosum suffers from arthritis,
but he continues to work.
His hands shake slightly,
almost imperceptibly.
For years, I didn't notice.

5.

Sometimes history
is a single sentence
spoken in the background
when you're on the phone
with someone else.
It makes for a terrible song.
I hear it sometimes,
then not at all.

6.

Silence is a room
where language
resides in the walls.
The subtle erasures
of childhood, the negative
space left behind by
lost sons, etc.

＊

I do not have
a mother tongue.
A mouth without
a mother tongue
speaks in echoes.
My words ricochet.
I chase after them,
even though
they're mostly
dying light.

7.

The Trans-Canada Highway
runs directly through my reserve,
splitting it in half, like a fruit
or a body on a surgical table.
A highway is less like a suture
and more like a wound.
In another reality, a reserve
could be a minor utopia, I think
every time I pass through my rez, visit family.
Heaven and God were good ideas.
Heaven is sorrow plus optimism
plus existential debt.

8.

The present consists
of that which precedes it.
It's simple, I know, but
this simplicity pains me.
Inside the past
are my family's memories.
Sometimes, without
warning, all the music
in me dies. Poof.
I am too young to have
to remember so much.

9.

When my kokum's mother died of COVID,
I watched the funeral on a livestream.
As our relatives prepared the casket for transport,
I heard sobbing. I knew it was her
even though she wasn't in the frame.
It's obvious: one can cry in a number
of grammatical tenses.
Throughout the entire service,
I had been listening in the past tense.

The Driftpile Cree Nation comprises approximately 15,000 acres of land on the southern shore of Lesser Slave Lake, the third-largest lake in Alberta. A "survey" was conducted in 1901 to establish its confines, after a Treaty Commissioner "laid out temporary Indian Reserves Boundaries for the Driftpile Band" in 1900.[ii] Prior to this, Cree leaders signed Treaty 8 on the shores of the lake on June 21, 1899. Representatives of the Crown oversaw the process. Due to acts of legal and linguistic trickery, the Treaty amounted to a cessation of territory and gave expression to "Her Majesty's . . . desire to open for settlement . . . a tract of country"[iii] much vaster than 15,000 acres—all of present-day northern Alberta.[iv]

Confession: I feel most Cree on the shores of the lake.

I feel held in all my complicatedness.

The horizon is a line of continuity between me and my ancestors—not unlike a line break.

I dream toward it.

As a boy, I waded in the water; I now realize that that was my first poem.

My small, trembling life is crouched in the margins of a veiled text that begins at the end of the 19th century.

My hypothesis: all the people of Driftpile were born in 1901.

1901 never ended. Tomorrow it will be 1901 again.

We are not citizens of a country.

We are citizens of a century.

CHILDHOOD TRIPTYCH

I.

In my first childhood home
on the reserve, where I lived with
my brother, the forest was visible
from a small window in the kitchen.
I imagine my father looked out that window
so as to escape himself. He would give us up
after about one year. I'm inclined to think
of that year as a landscape painting
that got repainted until all of it became
a blur of green. I get it now—my childhood
is an image of a forest someone else
was supposed to know by heart.

2.

What I don't know
about my childhood
doesn't destroy me.
The self emerges in
the absence of better
information. A native
childhood is the colour
of doubt. The colour of
doubt is blue. According
to plant scientists, blue
rarely occurs organically
in nature. When I write
about my parents in their
twenties, it is as though
I am writing about ghosts.
Can two ghosts produce
anything other than faded
memories? As a kid,
I had so much hope
I tried to sell it.
I now understand that
hope cannot be bought;
it is passed around,
like cutlery. Hope is not
abstract. It is solid, and
unbearable. It wounds.

3.

I used to think that the first tragedy of my life
was that I wasn't raised by my parents.
These days, I suspect that all children come
from the same country of dreaming. I didn't
so much leave as escape. My impulse was
to break open this poem. Like childhood.
To break something in order to repair it.
To touch all of the earth in order to think
about something else. I've forgiven everyone.
It's autumn already. So many leaves have fallen
—I have to go out and kiss each one.

THE CLOSET

after Lacie Burning's *Seeing in the Dark*

The body isn't really a trapdoor, but it is subterraneous.
When I was young I was already old. Who said that?[v]
So many hours spent in my bedroom, bearing myself.
I believed in debt because I wanted to be owed something,
because I lived against the grain of my own interior.
A brutal creativity I didn't choose. Some backstory:
people revisited the past, they set things down, aside, on fire.
One September, the day before school started, I fell
from my chapan's roof, a dizzy bird without wings.
I was a domestic subject, after all: I looked in the mirror
only when I wasn't thinking. The closet is such an ugly
metaphor; I wasn't actually invisible. What strange luck,
in the end, to be most yourself in the dark—
all that light churning inside you.

I haven't memorized enough about
the past. I remember someone else's
emotions, shapes, a rugged shoreline.
As a boy, I tried every week to not want
a different life. Language wasn't a burden
per se, but I was wet with it, I was shivering.
In a small way I had been insatiable. I had
too much hope. I didn't yet know that a native
person could be a poet, so I often went
to the water, its long edge a line breaking
at my exposed feet. From some dark
place inside me, some vacant chamber
of future thinking, a voice said, *Leap.*
So I leapt. I left.

We are not yet what we touch.
Our historical consciousness is a difficult dream;
the same way memory is an enduring indeterminacy.
It seems useful to open a book and traverse it.
The modern world: wow, gee.
Some men exude an alienating presentness.
There's no other way to put it.
I am constantly astonished; I am like a painting.
The clouds can be reshaped into two poets.
One is an old man who hums. The other is you.
In the field of thought-images I wasn't a failure.
Queerly, I favour tragedy over luxury.
The very idea of light must be worth something.
I must be something worth glancing at.

I must be something worth glancing at,
even if, like all natives, I begin in a text from the past.
I'm not naïve: North America doesn't exist.
Queer people will be free, the current political regime
will erode. History is a type of affective excess. It leaks,
like a long novel. Oh, the grandness of an unspectacular
Friday, a train barrelling toward a country of ecstasy.
I identify as an example of a quotidian life.
I experience bliss, I look happy in photographs.
What I need: a contagious happiness, an enclave
of the future, a force field around my heart.
The human condition is maniacal and oddball.
"Ephemeral traces" and "flickering illuminations" are
synonyms for the body. Rejoice: the present is a dead end!

What is a body in the present tense?
What is mourning but a queer fatherland
we can make claim to? I want to believe
in the possibility of an existing gay lifeworld,
but time is a form of bad faith. Once, I met up
with a man who refused to show his face on
the dating app. Kissing, he felt the small knife
in my pocket, but didn't care. My life is an auto-
biographical fiction. There is a section of my life
called "Great Anonymous Sex" and it's mostly lies
and awkward anecdotes. My redemption has been
lost and is yet to come. Still, I'd redo it all, if only
for the rare moments when, in the vista of a libidinal
economy, I was no longer an imprisoned subject.

In the prison house of the subject, I was economical.
I only wanted a song to sing on the dance floor
of a false reality. All natives live somewhere between
the modern and post-modern. Most days I'm a wind-up
man, waltzing into an account of time, space, presence,
absence, wholeness, etc. It is very human, the way
a man, during a threesome in Edmonton, left so that his
friend and I could better experience a reconstructed
intimacy. When I was younger, I sometimes logged on
to Grindr while visiting family in northern Alberta.
There were very few profiles, but most of them
belonged to other native men. One man told me he some-
times drove as long as four hours for a single, brief hookup.
We are meeting for the first time in this sonnet. *Hello*.

There are two kinds of sonnets: the ones we meet in
and the ones we leave behind. Is my life in fact historical
if I imagined I would be dead by now? What counts as
a queer poem? The poem thrumming in the air, like rain.
The poem I make of my hands when I hold the past
like a dead bird. I pretend I'm burying the past when
I'm actually burying myself. It's a game, we're at the
beach, and I'm not afraid to kiss my boyfriend in front
of homophobes, some of whom aren't really homo-
phobes, they just haven't refused a certain form of
finitude yet. Men represent a certain form of finitude.
Somehow, love is still a case study in singing. I'm less
so a man and more so a song or an edict. It took
just one man to invent me. I was a good idea once.

A man is a good idea when the lights are out and
your life feels amazingly painful. Oh faith, that
dysfunctional little house with shiny windows. Irony:
the last place I want to be is in a room full of men.
What if Muñoz is right and the world really is a degraded
zone of random violence? What shape must our poems
take? Maybe a sonnet can be a gay space that is weirdly
liberating. We all live on after our "dematerializations
as a transformed materiality." Our longings are so
rarely pure and simple. I love the small gestures that
permit us, I love being intent to be lost, I love how
much queer sense we make even when we're sad
and defeated. I have an inarticulate message for all
of you: to exist is a pain we have to keep bearing.

We all exist in painful proximity to the future.
Sadly, it never arrives. The present is full of people
without a future. I think utopia is the name
we give to the rooms in which we feel more
alive than dead. In one of my old bedrooms,
my bed sat in front of a huge mirror. Sometimes,
while having sex, I'd look at the mirror. Dear former
lovers, I'm sorry I was always finding ways to be
less present. I'm sorry that I was more aroused
by an image than real life. When I write about us
in the past tense we seem more alive. When I write
about us in the present tense the poem becomes
a eulogy. As far as I know, all of us are still living. It
doesn't have to hurt to dwell in someone else's image.

Indulging in the image of someone else's queer magnificence
can be a necessary act. My first time in a humble little
gay bar in Edmonton, I felt both true and not true.
The hum of other men's bodies was a decadence I didn't
at first understand. I left alone, blissed out in a dense presentness—
the banality of something I once thought unattainable. It is only now
that I realize utopia's rehearsal rooms were everywhere I went
as an extension of my repressed desires. The most important lesson
from those days was that a man's body could be a map to the world.
I barely survived, which feels indulgent to write from the luxury
of a coherent self. What can I possibly mean? Today I write
poems from the future. In the future, queer people are still
dying and dancing and feeling other people in dark rooms.
I linger on these things, so I know I must resemble my despair.

I don't want to linger on despair. Today,
I live and I work. I return to my homeland a bit
queerer, my heart exploding above me each time.
I dedicate my bold rebellions to the native men
left behind by history. I am most interested in
the archive as a question of whose hope gets
neglected, ignored. Like all queer natives, I tried
to turn to the past to envision a future. It was
both productive and unproductive, both
world-making and distracting. I have loved every
queer native man that I've met. It doesn't matter
if that is an exaggeration. To varying degrees,
we are all anachronistic. We are all myths whose
value will one day have their historical moment.

Regarding the moments of history that we continue
to relive, it can be hard not to be a little nihilistic.
The past is not an admirable text; it is a mausoleum.
I want to call attention to the dead, to the barely
living. I want to remind you of the gravity and
the challenge of responding to the world, of simply
being in the world. I became a homosexual because
pleasure was an aspiration, a structure of feeling I
knew as the vague shape of what would save my life.
I now know that to be a homosexual is to be a theorist
and an architect and an archivist and, of course, a poet.
We have to reject our negation, we have to harness
our love and joy in the act of utopian transformation.
Our social intercourse is not just some silly exchange!

Intercourse is so seldom a silly exchange.
I remember all the men I've slept with, if even
just the degree to which they amplified or eased
my loneliness. I belong to a circuit of dialectical
tensions between my friends and my sexual
acquaintances. Sometimes it is difficult to tell who has
altered me more. I would prefer to not become
a cheery anecdote. I want to be a vibrant and
aggressive collage! No one person is an artwork,
sadly. On the subject of dreaming, I was taught
to believe that my dreams were anticipatory, that
I could see into the future. I suppose it's not healthy
to focus on the literal collapse of our usual forms for
living, but what will be our new forms, our new fictions?

Fiction has a certain allure to me. Form and
content so rarely nourish one another in real life.
When I'm writing a novel, it seems the reader is
a fish I'm trying to transport in a small, clear bag
back to the river. Sometimes I read novels and
I'm like, *Does this book even care about real people
with real problems?* But I'm meandering now.
My childhood desires were depressingly simple.
I was not always certain that I wanted to be alive.
I was not a beautiful young man, and I had wanted
to be. I was large and introspective, always ruminating.
I loved to dream about how to liberate my nature.
But my youth in no way belonged to the mythopoetic.
It was a normal love I strived for. I did not get it.

I did eventually experience normal love.
Just before I started grad school, I dated
a man who texted me every evening for an
entire summer. We spent most weekends
together; we created our own pleasure principle,
our own interchangeable reality where every gesture
and gaze vibrated with a latent sexuality. I broke up
with him because he was sexting other men. I could not
imagine a nexus of erotic collaboration, I wanted
our world to be small and enchanted. In the private
room of contemplation that is a sonnet, I can
describe these previous chapters without shame.
My self-portraits are a little atypical, yes, a little
"wish-landscape," yes. Please, please forgive me.

I wished for a landscape of forgiveness, yes.
From Muñoz, I learned that the indentations
lovers left behind in my bed were legitimate
evidence of my own affective potentiality. I still
don't think we are in that unimaginable place
that is safe for men who desire men. Sure, the apps
turned the city into one big sexual fantasy, but
my suspicion is that there's something more
joyfully resonant out there, among flowers, in
the blurry horizon where revolution awaits us.
Sure, we have failed, but we have to keep imagining,
we have to keep exceeding our conditions of
possibility, late capitalism's usual formulations!
We can still become what we will one day touch!

I.

Someone lied to us—the body
isn't not a figure of speech.
I don't want anyone's sympathy.
I want a brief hour of rain between
hookups, a plastic boat called Grief
wide enough to sink in. Nothing excites
me as much as the possibility of transcending
history. Somehow, there are still
so many kinds of light.

2.

Once, a psychic told my mother
that I would get married,
have children. Alas! I'm not immortal,
all my sentences end in semicolons.
Even death is a beginning. What is the subtext
of my sadness? How do I live in the world
if I don't love it? Many days I'm hysterical.
I remember the wind and what the wind
rustles through. A man speaks to me
in a human voice. I try to admire what's
left of the future, which flickers.

"The too-closeness of the world," wrote Lauren Berlant.[ix]
We want a world but we can't bear it.

The anxiety to define my loneliness
but not transform it into property,

to find a place to think in without getting trapped.
What if love doesn't free me?

What if when my life ends there is still more life?

Not the man in the bed, at last,
who says "Don't worry, I'll be gentle,"
but the sweetness of my despair,
how it filled me up, like winter.
Like winter, I prized the catastrophe
of a new beginning. I kept forgetting
about the dynamics of desire. What do I do
with what men present as gentleness?
No one wants to be a historian of their
own marginalization, but here I am again,
hello. When I first moved to the west coast,
my kokum asked me if the grass had turned
brown yet. I said, "No, kokum, it stays green here
much longer." When she asked a second
time, I realized she was saying, "Somewhere
the earth is still green! We have not died yet!
The past isn't always at our feet!"

Suppose he doesn't
leave again. Suppose no
one else is coming
to save me. Suppose
love really is a willingness
to experience the same
disappointments, joys.
Confession: there are days
I can't resist identifying
with silence, with the deer
standing at the highway's edge,
so close to death that
the death seems complicit
with nightfall. How the deer
leaves the forest anyway.
Pathetic fallacy, pathetic
man, the cruelties of form,
and so on. Our language,
so worked over it is suddenly
gleaming again. Our bodies,
studied and rehearsed,
like common hymns.
Miraculously, some forms of sex
are akin to prayer.

"When your subjectivity feels loose,
let the world in, study the subjugated
knowledge of rain," I say to my students.
No one understands what I mean.
It is something like freedom—inhabiting
my own little sphere of nonsense ideas.
I am incumbent mayor and red ant and
total sunshine in the prairie of my ridiculous
consciousness. My people's homeland
has been categorized as both prairie and subarctic,
but it is actually a secret third thing.
We need fewer anthropologists and more
minor poets. "Here's to the eros of an adjective!"
I yell. "Here's to the golden age of having so little
to say and too many ways to say it!"
My students nod solemnly. *Silly man,*
I imagine them thinking, *does he know*
some people can only withstand
a tiny bit of love?

AUTOFICTION

If I place two imaginary
native people in a room,
what do they talk about?

The mouth is a kind
of stomach . . . Language
isn't really raw material . . .

I can't always discern my
audience. The living or the dead?
The happy or the unhappy?

My life takes up such native
themes as native interiority,
native thinking, native truth.

Texting a friend, I mistakenly
write: MY DEATH PERCEPTION
IS FAILING ME.

Ultimately, there is no such thing
as invented grief.

In a museum in Regina, there's a Treaty 8 archive, but the
accounts, apparently, are mostly incomplete.

For some reason, Regina feels years away, years too late.

Further, I too am incomplete.

I could book a flight this afternoon but people don't get
immediate access to archival materials, not even when
the materials involve their ancestors.

What if I make their memories into a museum?

What if doing so makes me even more lonely?

What if in the midst of too many objects I become one?

＊

Teaching, I tell my students that we use language in
ordinary ways to insist on our freedom.

Maybe this, I say, is "the lyric vernacular."

We make the earth signify with meaning in excess of conquest,
I think while driving home in the middle of a normal Friday
    afternoon.

✳

I mean to live more brilliantly but I'm on too many
    committees:
the committee on mixed metaphors, which is about the
    birds and their calamities;
the committee tasked with translating the rain, which is
    self-explanatory;
the political depression committee, where we argue over the
    best definition of "social realism."

✳

In my early twenties,
I had already breathed in
as much of the past
as was humanely possible.
Sometimes my desperation
was the size of a forest.
Sometimes I destroyed
what I didn't want stolen
from me.

✳

What is diffuse grief?

The window invents the bird's sense of scale.

What is an example of a living text?

*The weeds that grow uninhibitedly around the old residential
    school.*

What do the weeds believe?

That yesterday is a convenient concept.

✳

When I die, please recite the following: *When he was alive
he was sometimes beautiful. He dreamt about
a small corner of the earth, singing, and also dancing.
His biggest regret was that he wasn't the wind.*

My kokum texts me:
"lots of snow out here /
depression." Memory
is the distance between
two winters. We forget
what we're able to outlast.
Even the forest
has a language of its own.
By now, the aspens should
be bare. From some angles,
you can see from one end
of the forest to the other.
That is the forest speaking
in commas, its hushed
plea. It does not
address us. It addresses
the sky.

I treat the world
with a kind of critical
sincerity because
I know it can't possibly
last forever. Similarly,
I know I am a man
despite better options.
The longer I think
about the past
the less real I feel.
During the first
few months
of the pandemic,
I missed people
I hadn't seen
or thought about
in years. The way
I sometimes forget
I love the wind until
it's the middle of June
and I'm no longer
depressed. In years, it still
won't be the future.
The future is something
we leave behind, like gossip
or a library. My financial

advisor keeps encouraging
me to create a will, but
I hate thinking about
the heavy luggage
of my daily life.
I could ride the trend
of reckless optimism
for a while; too bad I am
easily frightened,
like a horse that
expects an ambushing.
I think I still want what
I always wanted:
to spend enough time
with a man that
our days become
something like a long,
meandering sentence.
All we would need
is a single comma
to continue living.

I experience an afternoon so empty
I pretend my whole life hasn't
consisted of one long Blue Period.
At times, I had a use for my world-
weariness; my minor longings seemed
so enormous. The hardest task of my early
twenties was to withstand myself.
I imagine my exes thought I spent a lot
of time ambling around my apartment,
and they were right. I like the word "amble"
because it belongs to the horses.
What if I belong to the horses, the pre-contact
ones scientists assumed didn't exist?
When I was in Europe, people assumed
I didn't exist. Some French people refused
to speak to me in English, and how
could I blame them? Last week, I read
a novel that argued rational thought
has always been used to convince us
we're worthy of salvation
despite the counterevidence. I write poems
to remind myself I am in love with a freedom
I haven't yet experienced. I have plenty
material pleasures, yes, but they are
almost all coping mechanisms. I can't
help it—all day I keep wanting to be saved.

What others call Sentimentality
I call Refusing to Suffer Alone.
I was so overwrought with imagining
it was hard to think—a funny fate
for a poet. Do the stars know that
we can't redeem them? (An old question.)
What does it mean that they still call
out for us? Is each poem a kind
of calling outward from a place
near death? On some maps, there
are the republics of Poetry and Death
and all that's between them is a lush forest.
That forest is called Listening Carefully.
The point is to get lost,
become a tree.

THE PROBLEM WITH PLEASURE[x]

after David Garneau

Most days I've wanted
to be my desires and not merely
the unrelenting density
from which they rush forth.
The problem with pleasure is that
two people can meet in a room
in order to exist less. It's not that
I disliked myself; it's that no one
told me it was possible to feel
that much of the world all at once.
I felt everything, I was constantly
coming apart, like an orange, half-
peeled on the table, a life split
in two ways: toward the past, which
I couldn't free myself from, and
toward the future, which is to say,
toward both ecstasy and pain.
At some point I decided
there was no use in parsing
the difference.

> *"But we may say that about Lesser Slave Lake there are stretches*
> *of country which appear well suited for ranching and mixed*
> *farming; that on both sides of the Peace River there are extensive*
> *prairies and some well wooded country; that at Vermilion, on the*
> *Peace, two settlers have successfully carried on mixed farming on*
> *a pretty extensive scale for several years, and that the appearance*
> *of the cultivated fields of the Mission there in July showed that*
> *cereals and roots were as well advanced as in any portion of the*
> *organized territories. The country along the Athabasca River is*
> *well wooded and there are miles of tar-saturated banks."[xi]*
>
> From settler correspondence relating to the
> negotiation of Treaty 8 in northern Alberta, 1899

I.

On both sides of the river I wept.

Sometimes language is an unorganized territory. Sometimes
    it is a tar-saturated bank.

Settlement is a problem for interpretation.

In July, it was hotter than it's ever been in my kokum's lifetime.

She has only left northern Alberta once. I have left too
    many times.

2.

 we may say that ▮▮▮▮▮▮▮▮▮▮▮▮ there are

some well wooded

years,

3.

in all of us.

An invisible war but the soldiers are everywhere.

No bombs because they planted them inside us already.

In the middle of the night, the sun materialized on the bedroom walls, beams of light shooting out from God's fists.

Dear God, why does the rain fill me up so fast?

And when will we come up with another word for salvation?

I met the Minister of Loneliness and even he was drowning.

Don't worry, my love.

All our parents are emigrants from a wounded century.

Please keep me company in these rare hours during which we truly see each other.

Most of us have 20th-century faces;
time cleaves to us like frost.

*

From photographs I try to retrieve
a trace of lost narrative, but memory
isn't imagistic. It is the atmosphere.

*

Nostalgia is not nothing.
I remember the old silence.
Years accrue inside me
like hay bales. The hay is made
from words. The words are all
from another country.

*

When there are no monuments
where you come from,
everything lives in the throat.

*

I tried to write with my throat,
but the trees in me
grew denser.

*

Two men huddle together
on a frozen lake, like a couplet.
If I cut them out of the landscape,
I'd be left with the sky, a blank page,
generalized suffering.

*

The men rattle around
in the dark like abstract
ideas, their pants unspooling
into dreams, their dreams
unspooling into antiquity.

*

Let solitude wreck me.
The earth is inside my shirt.

Because it's the coldest December
on record, I haven't left my mother's
house in over a week. I love how simple
it is to live right now (it so rarely is), how
small and inconsequential my desires are
(which rarely are). It would be easy to continue
on in this way—hemmed in on all sides by bright
light. At last, Lord, the whiteness of the world
doesn't frighten me. At last, Lord, I am not
my anguish. Outside the window, a row of poplars
sway at the edge of a tiny schoolyard. Each a statue
of awe. Each stunned by its own capacity for survival.
Because I was so sad all the time, I used to think, like
the famous poem, that I was in the winter of my life,
but I was wrong. I saw the whole world and still ached
for my childhood, which was half-mystery, half-omen.
It isn't that death is a resolution, but one day I too
will be buried beneath snow. Somehow,
this explains everything.

NOTES

i. "painfully available" is Roland Barthes' phrase, *Mourning Diary*.

ii. https://www.transcanadahighway.com/listing/driftpile-cree
-nation/.

iii. https://www.rcaanc-cirnac.gc.ca/eng/1100100028813
/1581293624572.

iv. This deceit would prove costly for the entire planet, northern
Alberta being the site of the infamous Oil Sands.

v. In *The Lover*, Marguerite Duras wrote, "One day, I was already
old." I misremembered it as what appears in the poem.

vi. Commissioned by the Words on the Water Campbell River
Writers' Festival in 2024.

vii. I wrote these sonnets by gathering keywords and phrases in
José Esteban Muñoz's *Cruising Utopia: The Then and There of
Queer Futurity* and building around them. The aim wasn't
merely to replicate Muñoz's language (though at times I do),
but rather and more difficultly to collaborate with the text so
as to make something distinct, so as to create a plural voice
with a mixed autobiography.

viii. Adapted from a poem I wrote in response to T.S. Eliot's *The
Waste Land*, commissioned by the Toronto International
Festival of Authors.

ix. Lauren Berlant's "A Properly Political Concept of Love."

x. First published in *Dark Chapters: Reading the Still Lives of
David Garneau.*

xi. https://www.rcaanc-cirnac.gc.ca/eng/1100100028813
/1581293624572.

ACKNOWLEDGEMENTS

Much gratitude, as always, to Cody and Stephanie, for being my guides.

Thank you to the students in my poetry classes, who helped stir my poetic imagination even when I was writing in other modes.

Thank you to everyone at McClelland & Stewart, Carcanet Press, and Beacon Press for welcoming me and this book into your beautiful orbits. Thanks, especially, to Canisia Lubrin for her editorial insights.

Thank you to the journals that published earlier versions of some of these poems, including *Arc Poetry Magazine*, *Yarrow Magazine*, *Denver Quarterly*, and *The Walrus*.

BILLY-RAY BELCOURT (he/him) is from the Driftpile Cree Nation in northwest Alberta. He won the Griffin Poetry Prize for his debut collection *This Wound is a World*. He has twice been nominated for the Governor General's Literary Award—once in poetry for the debut and in non-fiction for his memoir, *A History of My Brief Body*. Both his works of fiction, *A Minor Chorus* and *Coexistence*, were national bestsellers. He is an Associate Professor in the School of Creative Writing at the University of British Columbia.